Woodworking And Places Near By

Carol Cox

Hanging Loose Press

Published by Hanging Loose Press
231 Wyckoff Street
Brooklyn, NY 11217

Some of these poems first appeared in the following publications:
Epoch, Foxfire, The Greensboro Review, Hanging Loose and
Southern Exposure. "Watching You Draw" and "From the Direction
of the State Mental Institution" appeared in the Crossing Press
anthology, *Mountain Moving Day,* edited by Elaine Gill. The quotation
from Wendell Berry is in *Openings,* New York: Harcourt Brace
Jovanovich, 1968; the quotation from Lorine Niedecker is in *The
Collected Poems (1936-1966),* Penland, North Carolina: The Jargon
Society, 1968.

Cover by Ronnie Lindsey.
Book design and layout by Larry Zirlin.
Typeset by Jeffrey Schwartz.

Hanging Loose thanks the National Endowment for the Arts for grants in
support of this project.

Library of Congress Number 78-529-22.
ISBN 0-914610-13-9.

Produced at The Print Center, Inc., Box 1050, Brooklyn, N.Y.,
11202, a non-profit printing facility for literary and arts-related
publications. Funded by The New York State Council on the
Arts and the National Endowment for the Arts.

for Fletcher

CONTENTS

I. Places Near By

9   After the Tornado, the Weather Turned Very Cold
10   Watching You Draw
11   Down the Road
12   Cedar Tree Outside My Study
13   If We Could Gather In
14   Departure
15   Late Summer
16   Looking Forward to Winter
17   Aging
18   Lifting
19   The Cat with Meningitis
20   The Territory Ahead
21   Opening
22   The Attic
23   Since I Have Known You, I Have Known You Will Leave
24   Drought
25   Missed Connection
26   From the Direction of the State Mental Institution
27   Two, Crossing
28   Wedding Trip to the Outer Banks
29   Getting Ready
30   The Visitor
31   Listening to James "Son" Thomas Sing Delta Blues
32   Poem for F.
33   Wrappings
34   When the Light Falls
35   Planning a Field of Sunflowers
36   Asking for Directions
40   Working In
41   Lines
42   Reconciliations
43   Constancy
44   Greens

II. Woodworking

49 The Wood: Cherry
50 Secrets
51 Coming Up from the Marsh, I See My Shop Lit Up
52 Night: 1
53 Night: 2
54 Vases
55 Several Have Started
56 Sawdust
57 Three Stories About Wood
58 Pricing Your Goods
59 Resumption
60 Burls
61 Resting
62 Waking
63 Mistake
64 In the Workshop
65 Friends Dropping By

I

Places NearBy

In the heron's eye
is one of the dies of change.
Another is in the sun.
Each thing is carried
beyond itself.

—Wendell Berry
"Window Poems"

AFTER THE TORNADO,
THE WEATHER TURNED VERY COLD

the sky gleamed,
        light through a bottle,
then the warm wind
tucked under,
rolled away.

a few people stood about
in the mud,
their heads tipped down,
occasionally bending over
and whispering, long blank ribbons of sound.

then the sky iced over
and pushed down hard again,
forcing the coldness of wings
and limbs and breath
under the pitted blankets
that were left,

that were freed from owners
and scattered like stiff bright leaves
around the trees.

WATCHING YOU DRAW

Bent over those
dark threads of ink,
your back is thin and fair

as a cattail
leaning under the weight
of a red-winged blackbird.

The old lamp I read under
sends you smoking colors
you do not need but use,
folding them into
your shadowed corner.

Your back is a network
of hollow birds,
false gold,
and marginal lines held tight across
the throats of pretenders.

DOWN THE ROAD

The ditches on either side
lift above the gravel

cows block the way, their blotched
winter hides hanging in the air
       like frozen bark

wire twists through the mud pools,
gleaming in the last
sharp bits of light

a tractor rumbles off toward
the latest accident

The sun is going down

I dig small holes in the yard,
for bulbs,
in case nobody comes

CEDAR TREE OUTSIDE MY STUDY

(the needles curving slowly
into fingers over my forehead

that dark, dark green
cutting a path in and through):

I always think it is a human shape
dwarfed, hulking, when I come in
and lift the shade;
the difficulty is
I cannot smell through glass,
and in this room
heated by false fire and
        rimmed with books of poems,

nothing is rare.

IF WE COULD GATHER IN

A bowl holds fifty cracks,
none leaks: the streaks are rich
as scars, playing back
the calm sound of growing
for a reason. After all, clay lies
in the throat of my dead child-niece,
sends bulbs shooting through
a flooding river bed: needed diversions.

Fear of the unknown comes down
hard as hatred of the known.
The translation is not movable.
If we could gather in over an acre of ground,

we would not need to be solid,
or to worry about it;
we could invent our own
diseases and economy,
and then dismiss them lightly.

DEPARTURE

Eleven o'clock: my brother and sister
are gone,
hurled back into the sky
to be dropped among gold Georgia fruit.

I can leave their faces,
can take up the cat
and sail around the silent house
touring the plants.

Photographs are too rare to be looked at,
anyway;
there's much that needs doing—
this gazing and thinking's no good.

But I feel as though I have on blinders
made from scraps of sun,
as though my cheeks may burst
from too much heat,

and the door coming open
is what I need,
is all I will allow.

LATE SUMMER

Growing older in August
seems unfair;
the dry walls of the body
need the strength of young animals
only two months in the field.
The day is a journey into heat,
a remove from shallow pools
the mind sorts out in liquid rows.

The night leaves me more alert than tired
and soon a sense of loss grows in:
windows kicked out and
        lying ragged on the grass.

But:
the fear of fire is an excuse only.

15

LOOKING FORWARD TO WINTER

The house will suck in cold
wet air,
layer our ankles, our mattress on the floor.
Pine needles will choke the gutters,
flumes for our only water.
The road will sink.

A house that is an island
knocking up out of its own skeleton
is the shelter we have lifted
out of our skins,
by choice,
a familiar vein in a nonessential body.

We are iron figures
through the doors,
measuring the walls that clamp shut
with the message of fourteen hour dark,
        feeling between the pictures
        for a passage lit by stone flares.

AGING

he has held on so long
that the ropes slipping down
leave nothing but frayed bone

the ropes going into the earth
a life of their own
know the simple gaps
between rocks

he has leaned down looking
but the wind folding over
        like a heavy screen
has lifted the choices
has sealed the joints

LIFTING
for Charles and Pat
on their wedding day

The woods this year
are warm and bright;
we have lived the winter
in rain and green buds
lifting from the corners of the yard.
We have drowsed under cotton blankets
brought from my grandmother's house.

Frightening almost—
     summer stamped over November
     like hot wax
     and now a vague brown autumn
     wearing through January,
     neither dead nor licensed to live—
except that friends I know
understand and teach
how waiting,
waiting for the cold
to come, descent of death,
is negative use of the mind,
energy burned and gone.
Plants, they show, know more.

They are in the spare room
lifting maps onto new walls,
watching the sun spread over
lines that used to be in shadow,
seeing which window holds the north.
Tonight the weather forecast,
late supper and wine;
tomorrow a winter marriage. The
quince blooms as it rarely has before.

18

THE CAT WITH MENINGITIS

Her brain damaged,
the disease just beginning
to leak away,
she tries to re-learn
the use of her legs,

sleek black legs
giving like water,
bent out of shape
and denied all but ground space,
dark head angled
so that feet and doors
float, are not where they were before.

She sits by the kitchen door
where the outside hangs in her loose memory,
howls in anger
at the distance of the tall grasses:
her field thick with light
        and small animals
plowing along at enormous speeds.

THE TERRITORY AHEAD

His legs were driven down;
knit, cold mineral,
into the clay pastures of south Mississippi.

We did not know they were hidden.

Our duty was seeing the whole figure,
smiling at the success of integration.

We think of going to the farm
where it happened,
so that we can end it
with some attitude of motion.
We want to remember songs
we heard ten years ago.

But we are too startled
to break pattern right now;
too much might be missing.

The gunshot might be missing:
the first noise of the night,
riding up our backs,
inaccessible.

OPENING

The moon points south, leaving me behind.

Flakes of light across the floor
begin to fade in-
to the crusted wood,
leaving edges like brown salt.

I open them up, break them open
like tender eggs:
hear you whispering in the corners
dissolving my ears
with stories of where the light goes.

THE ATTIC

It is a left space,
        hung between delicate snares,
a gleaming rusty twilight
any hour of the day,
seeming to grow slowly inward,
its ragged beams
a subtle pressure on the oiled wood below.
People avoid it, needing reasons.
Familiar and old as a water-stain,
it has occupied an unforgivable zone.

When the first noises
come clattering out,
the men up and down the road
lift their eyes in fear.
The women all sitting in the rooms
under the attic
look into the mirrors of each other's hands,
no less or more moved than in the past,
feeling the absent beats,

the curtains drawing themselves open

SINCE I HAVE KNOWN YOU,
I HAVE KNOWN YOU WILL LEAVE

for Fran and Paul

Splinters are clear,
at least,
dark sharp bits ,
filling up my thumbs.
An irritant I can live with,
(like the smell from the
country sewage system)
because I love the wood.

Your back is a vague form,
the dark green of a turtle's back,
the shadow of bark.
It has been turning
for two years;
I recognize myself in it.
I recognize all of us,
planted among the pebbles
on the road,
backs turning
like roots searching for water:
and I wish
for a sure, clean pain,
a diamond
twisting into the heel.

DROUGHT

If the rain pulls back in
this time
we will have to recognize the dark streams
that lie just too far
below the trees
and must be spaded up

the water that passes under us
while we sleep
and is vanishing
as I think I hear it
flooding out a stale dream

At the ends of those nights
you wander about
exhausted eyes shifting to the windows
drained hands measuring the clouds

MISSED CONNECTION

the porch swings
between ferns

the ferns thick as foam and
green,

the roots like brown threads
flowing out;

they need protection through the winter.
I had watched

for the cold weather,
my ears pressed to the changing

wind, my fingers
resting on the tin watering can

in the slim wave of sunlight.
(But the motion of the porch,

the stillness of the ferns
left me in confusion, and

I lost touch,
first with the weather,

then with the doors
that kept banging

somewhere off to the side.)

FROM THE DIRECTION
OF THE STATE MENTAL INSTITUTION

comes a crackling noise, a kind of chirping
which you can't hear any better
if you put your ear to the ground,

and then you might be rolled
into a category and stamped
with a capital letter. but meanwhile

the noise prevents sleep, follows
just far enough away
to stick like sap. you will

do anything except go nearer,
you will recite poems you don't
even know loudly and offer

proposals of marriage to faces
which keep trying to place you.
that is the end

of the story of your life
out on the sidewalk on an empty spot
near which ants have planted

tiny points of old food.

TWO, CROSSING

He brushes cottonseed out of his joints
and squints at my lettuce rows,
parsley, gourds.
He is surfacing that bulging earth,
I am looking for a way down.
He writes in the dirt
why some things didn't come up,
smoothing the rotted beans onto his palms,
carrying stalks away
inside his arms. The slice of sun
over his head burns hotter than over mine,
a terrifying energy
like sap loose from a young tree.

When we have finished crossing
back and forth over the rows,
we rest beside the blackberry growth
where leaves and flowers are ripe
and good for a new meal.

WEDDING TRIP TO THE OUTER BANKS

I

There were good reasons,
and so it was done.

The water breaks
across my forehead;
hours have a strange new use.

II

She will think for long afternoons
about building along
the edge of the water.
Each second will be clear,
perfect;
and her fingers will be long enough.

III

We have seen a strange legend
upon the ocean:
a lost captain dancing in his rowboat,
dreaming of pirates.

That is how we finally met.

GETTING READY

My own death weighs in
lengthy, disjointed

when the rain slides to an end
leaving the cistern full
and a dripping sound like footsteps
crashing over the moonless night

when the elderberries sink to the ground
fevered, rotting
feeding the earth for the next season
and the birds lift out what they can
pockets of darkness in the still light

when you sit in the field
gathering weeds as graceful as sculpture
which will shatter
out of your pots on the windowsill

it stretches past my ankles,
a stainless gesture,
is gone:

when the meeting leaves my skin
tender and familiar
as your legs are settling over mine,
as the yard is where we plant and water
dogwood, unnamed vines—
I will know that the uses of things
have been made clear and relentless
and it will be right
whether I step out
east or south.

THE VISITOR

I am shaken from rare afternoon sleep.
Sheltered in cotton scarves,
a girl rocks shyly outside the screen
dull with hope
that I will read the print
squeezed across her yellowed cards.
She whispers about Jesus.

The screen is jammed with insects.
A rising storm yanks loose dry grass.
I have lost the moment
of coming out of dreams.

She watches the wind,
clutching at her scarves.
Her hands move like small brown animals.
She knows where she will go
when the rain comes.

I hear myself saying,
Yes, yes, I will,

into the dark afternoon,
a cave where the river is rising,
into eyes black and empty of pretense
as soldiers cutting through a jungle night.

LISTENING TO JAMES "SON" THOMAS
SING DELTA BLUES

I think of blooming roots,
                    waking spiders,
       bulky rusting stems;
of the digging and sorting
spring will do
if left alone.

Son Thomas singing on this
watery March night,
       thick enough to fill up warehouse doors,
fine screens built all over town
to keep out growth:

he tells us what it is
       he's broken open every hour,
but not how many silver fingers
were replaced
after the ruin became too clear.

POEM FOR F.

Digging your heels in
under the sky
        you have turned up a new place.
The ants fly away. An old root,
brown scrap of bone, sifts through.
        The fig trees won't live,
it's too late in the year:
the heat presses against sore feet.

You bring up rotting leaves
to mash around the twigs,
        working your hands to the tune
from the radio in the window.
        Your eyes, under the sky,
watch for dark clouds.

The yard is full of small trees,
        leafing sticks,
in various stages of life and death.

(Waiting for You to Come Home)

This time is wrapped
in tight paper, old string,

knocks my ankles as I go by,
insists on being written down.
Dead moths coat the bottom
of my pencil cup. Notebooks rattle.

Hurrying outside to get the shovel and hoe
out of the weather,
I am caught in the magic of the warm wind.
The persimmons have fallen.
The first doves are dying in the woods.

When your truck hurls up the drive
I am gripped in a moment of panic
at the time I have lost,
start forward and then hold back,
frozen like a sad deer in the headlights.

But you notice the different shape of the house
right away.

WHEN THE LIGHT FALLS

When the light falls

the room, vacant
    except for my poems lining the walls
    (shields against nightmares)

breaks up into chambers
of thumping insects, green flecks
                  fat brown wings
colliding against my open eyes
tangling in the bit of gold
around my neck

reversed creatures,
come looking for a darker spot

or else
my consciousness of light
whited out their blots against the walls.

I feel my hands
breaking through the sheets
pushing away the full air
turning on all the lamps
in the house
    a lit field on the brown road

back in the room
the scraping noise
might be your hand
    drifting over the floor
or mice opening remembered places
or that shelf, sleep,
cracking in preparation

PLANNING A FIELD OF SUNFLOWERS

The seeds lie
in the lines of my hands

the washing goes on
and the rearranging

and I spend the light hours
thinking of the top of Vincent's head

lifting off,
the sunflowers moving in

(later there is a burial nightmare
so that I can wake

to the southern winter rain
covering December like a coat of hair;

I have to wait for an hour in March
just after rain-darkness and before full sun

the scattering has to be casual
my hands already in yellow shadow
                            with black nails

I have to refuse to look
when I feel the ground slant
                            and cats leap away:

the bowls in my house are full of water
and the oven is heating up.

ASKING FOR DIRECTIONS

in memory of Marti 1943-1972
Andrea 1969-1972

I. After, He Lies in the Hospital

They have come:
behind wretched hours
of long southern farms and slick
     night-lit corridors;
they spread out through the gathered blood,
tender as a fan, ribbed
and blinding.

(Just as the water
lies away from itself,
edging back from the fishes
it became,
that still and certain promise.)

In the blank soundless bed
he moves dimly,
so utterly changed, so far away
that he is delivered instantly
back into their bodies,

his thin stinging force
met with an outrage
only he can understand
and welcome.

The locked and speechless moon
circles past that room
in a set they know now, perfectly;

they cover his bed with split hands,
shining tissue,

until he calls back, finally,
past the stainless halls,
                    revolving sky,
in a hungry, ripened voice.

II.

A pipe lies somewhere on this killing,
killing road. A toy.

They do not belong in the grasses,
will not smooth out,
press down,
will not fill up with rain.

The sun will turn them
laboring into the eyes

of hidden walkers
who are ready but do not know

who will fall back
into the steaming side woods,
                    the southern forest,

into that wide, fine, black
simple apparition.

III.

> *this is her twenty-ninth year*
> *this is her third year*

I know at last how far
outside I was;

soft as grapes
those lovely word-streets,
dusky, sinking backyards
I lingered in.

After the burial
I will hone myself,
a pearl-strip cutting across
the dreams of my brother
and leading back home,

a lean accurate sign
of choices,
of how the weather will take shape.

IV. Last Visit in Detroit

Moving deep into the smoking rimless city
where summer festivals jam against
the hot wind

she carried her blessed dark-haired child
to offer her in measures of noisy
anxious love

to blur the edges of the streets, the river
rocking against the left-over
outlines of us all

Years ago in a night full of sweet poison
she was locked up in eyeless Birmingham
slept in the wood of the church
prayed in a hall of drowning ears

a night sloping down like this one
blackening Detroit
when the child watched the festival vanish
after it was ridden

she watched the child
the limping city-neighbors
the beaten starlight

saw her arms turning stiff and golden
and started the new tools
in a mud-slanted lot
        south of the cordoned blocks
        near the house where people
        flowed in and out
        asking for directions

Mounds of pecans, hard brown pellets,
lie inside an old straw basket
on the grey porch steps.
Long, fuzzy leaves of mustard greens
fan thickly out on newspaper
damp with falling dew.
The pine straw has been gathered
and sawdust swept from the workroom
for scattering through the garden.

There's nothing left to the day.

I wander across the dark spaces
where the tilting sun's blocked by leaves,
my body a thin line of light,
my mind dropping crinkled bulbs around
so the spring yard will wash up
speckled red.

Thinking there's a noise,
I go inside.
The walls draw in as though
they had relaxed while I was gone.
The rooms fall silent and cold,
and I know it is time to settle myself
for the night, to bring my hands
all the way in,
to learn each room again.

There's nothing breathing here.

What is it that I want to be alive?
These poems blown up across the page?

Lighting the gas heat,
I startle the spiders
into gulping their prey.

LINES

The line of the cat's mouth
is the curve of salted land
where the lake dries up

the smile of an ancestor
hidden in a foreign wind
racing past
and settling

RECONCILIATIONS

I believe she's dead (the neighbor's child)
and I know this cool morning
is wrong for August.

One of the corn plants toppled
during the night;
the others keep growing,
wooing circles of bees,
and are twelve feet high.

I must say to myself,
it's all right, it's safe:

the closing of the gate when
        there is no sound,
a scraping noise in the middle
        of an open field.

CONSTANCY

The lady next door grows herbs
in a spot of sunshine
by her window; nearly every morning

her cat kills a bird.
Once she offered me a glass of port
and mentioned her childhood
on a farm in Kansas:
she said, sometimes at night
my mouth felt so filled with wheat
that I spent hours drinking water
instead of sleeping.

When her hair had turned white
one morning, she brought me
one of her paintings: a field of wheat.
I should have known,
for the cat had already gone,
leaving a few small bones
scattered over the yards.

GREENS

From the tilting stones behind the porch
slit open by the evening light,
I watch you bending over
in the garden
sorting out greens for our autumn meal.

Wood chips from the day's work
darken your hair;
oil stains twist around your jeans.

In the house stands a table well-made:
tightly joined,
cherry gleaming like old sunlight.
You have hated it and made it your child,
cursed it in your dreams and
felt the pores in your hands
opening like the ones in wood.

At this moment
you have only to think about food,
the shaking off of dirt and worms,
the pulling of onions.
Yet this too holds you:
the soil's needs,
the problem of wild plants
that may be edible going to waste.
The garden moves around you,
rising and settling as you attend
to each matter that needs your thought.

You stand, gazing at the earth,
as the last light drifts out.

I give you a moment of letting down:
then call,
can see your smile flow out,

and you are coming up,
arms and mind full,
ready for supper
or a change in weather
or the silence of the house.

I snap on the kitchen light.
You begin to wash the greens.
The luxury is thick,
warm on this bare floor;
deep,
the cistern after a storm.

II

Woodworking

My friend tree
I sawed you down
but I must attend
an older friend
the sun
—Lorine Niedecker

THE WOOD: CHERRY

Bright cherry rings the house,

circles your face.
When I glance over,
I cannot understand what I see.
The gouge slips,
and my finger gleams red,
hovers in pain over the wood.

Almost no one else
loves the natural shade as you and I do;
for years they have tried to turn it brown.

I do hate the blood though,
and want to turn my eyes somewhere else
until the episode is over.

SECRETS

small ebony ellipse
I can shape you into a box
for holding tiny pins
or golden eyes

your cleared space
as wide and bright as water
lures me
as water does
promising sun-hard rocks
near the edge only
an entry metal-smooth

I know where the tablet of instructions is buried

COMING UP FROM THE MARSH,
I SEE MY SHOP LIT UP

The smell of smoke from the morning's trash burn
lurks in my coat.
There will be sleet tonight, heavy cold,
and new sounds of mice scattering across the kitchen floor.

I stop beside the garden
where slender onion stalks and thick bluish kale
lean slightly in the winter light.

The window is clouded with webs
left over from summer
and with stacks of dust.
It tells great stories; I can't wait to go in.

Fletcher, wearing wool shirts,
works on his chair in a room clogged with machines.
Later I may visit him
and tell him my new scheme
for the placing of legs. I can hear
his laughter now,
steering outside and curving around
to crack against the window of my shop.

NIGHT: 1

In bed,
the work is left behind
and brought still closer in.

I know that in my dreams
new shapes evolve,
sculptures done in heavy purple woods
and pale wood light as a star.
I know that you will think all night
about how long the joints will hold
and when and how you came to love
the wood so much.

Against you and away from you
under this dark green blanket
I know that any work is possible

and likely to be done
when there is light enough.

NIGHT: 2

Splinters of walnut
scrape across the sheet
and settle in my skin.

I wake up laughing at the wound:

here is my dream—
      body clogged with sawdust,
      pitted with chips,
      and pierced by glittering tools!

The sun this morning is a thin edge of oak,
golden and knot-hard.

VASES

I have learned to fashion
small, curved vases
from thin strips and thick slabs
of wood, to cut and shape
and polish with fine paper
until the piece gleams like a jewel.
I have come to know a little about direction of grain
and strength.
I have learned to look carefully,
face near the ground,
for delicate weeds, dark brown and cream,
to decorate my work.
I have seen how one's breath
can be closed up inside a solid block,
turned into the gift of loss,
a solemn nourishment.

SEVERAL HAVE STARTED

Several have started
to find such a life
as they thought we had,
but they poked their fingers
around the faces of clocks
and kept bumping into
the day's tin corners.

. . . .

The hours wind around my legs
and give me fresh strength,
a link,
the will to knock off numbers
unless their shapes are beautiful
and rare.
At night I peel away articles of time
and speak,
even if the room is empty.

. . . .

All the rooms are filled with layers
of work and pleasure.
My fingers, sanded numb,
have never been so dear.
Once someone heard me picking up
a small, delicate saw,
but when I turned to explain its use,
he was gone.

SAWDUST

Around the garden,
piles of sawdust in this pattern:

walnut, cherry, ash;
mahogony, maple, beech.

On this pale, cloudy day
the rich colors
lie like a sand painting:
I am in a painted desert,

here,
standing barefoot in a patch of mint,
before a storm that will go on for days,
deep in the south country.

Fire ants stir beneath the warm chips
and the dust on top blows up
into a wet wind.

THREE STORIES ABOUT WOOD

Zebrawood

A smooth circle of zebrawood
lying in your palm
polishes the skin
until it's a new place;

your enemies could set fire to the hand,
even,
and you would go on smiling.

Padauk

There's no other red like this.

Strangers coming in to gaze at it
feel their feet sink and catch;
then notice that the room
is worn in rich, dark color,
unattended fires,
bruised birds lining the blank walls.

Bubinga

As long as the tools are sharp—
the purple curves,
the pale,
the brown,
the lovely pale purple-brown
can live forever on my bench.

I'll carve it into my own shadow
and learn to live off smoke.

PRICING YOUR GOODS

Maybe there will be a new mushroom by your doorstep,
a tongue with a new word.

Maybe you will find a dance which needs curved legs,
a bone which ties a knot.

Do we have to wait?
Bring what you have

and we'll run a festival of trades,
a fair where ordinary sums

become fantastic, whisk the mind
into a zone of closed storage,

warehouses built of silver brick.

RESUMPTION

Coffee cups, brown glaze on white,
stand along the bench.
Spilled liquid leaves clumps of grey sawdust
around unfinished work.
The tools are dull,
and I have sat on my crooked stool for hours
trying to think of mirror designs.

A friend comes by to see how the work goes,
to share new books,
to drink tea from an ivory cup.
I pick up a slipstone,
and we whisper through the afternoon.

BURLS

The tree covers its wound,
builds a hard shell over infection,
the chance of rot.
Sliced, the knotty grain is dazzling—
deep, silky whorls of gold and rust.

My last feast will be set
with priceless bowls.

RESTING

Your body rests along a plank.
The late morning sun spreads out,
    a fine yellow wash,
tender and light after three days of rain.
The tin cistern, abandoned,
has ruptured in various places
and dribbles rain water into the softened yard.
The cat has found a brick
where she can dry her feet;
she disappears in a clump of wild onion blooms.

Leaning against the back steps,
I push my feet slowly
through the damp wood sorrel.

The mockingbirds dip recklessly
through each other's territories
and young plants heave up the garden.
    For a moment I lose focus:
it is hard to know
whether stillness or motion predominates;
it is hard to know where you are precisely,
though I can see points along your skin.

It is hard to imagine
what new fine, smooth object
will be resting in the finishing room
at the end of a long afternoon's work.

WAKING

There's a turn in this day
that I dreamed of, though
it was disguised as night:

I remembered (when I woke at four,
clicked the light, and
scratched down a line of poetry)

the huge maple block
waiting to become a bowl.

Standing now in the hall
in a thin gown,
I find words chipping off my fingers,
powdered steel and skin
salting the dark boards.

MISTAKE

The sorrow of work broken
in a careless moment
is a metal trap hung above the hands,
a dream of terrifying possibilities.

I have cheated,
and gone to stand in the soaking weeds
near the marsh.
The cows will be moving up to drink,
and dragonflies print clear threads of blue
on the milky air.

My body shakes,
and shakes,
and gives no sign of leaving off.

IN THE WORKSHOP

I keep note paper near.

I keep a hand-blown glass near,
      heavy and filled with water,
      and a clay bowl full of dried fruit.

I keep a brown cotton cloth near,
      thin and soft,
      for cover.

The cat is near,
      and the screens let in green weather
      and the odor of pear trees.

My hands explode with so many things to do;
I may still be counting them off
at bedtime
if I need to rest before sleep drops down.

FRIENDS DROPPING BY

Their faces seem dark,
for I have been lost in the work
and for a moment cannot find my way back;
my hands shake slightly
from gripping the tool.

Coming from a place where
talking is the order of the day,
they settle in,
ears and mouths glittery with expectation.

I can serve cold tea and almonds,
now,
I can move between the rooms
and F. can smile at them—
    the afternoon light lifts gold strips
    across our faces—
we can form a slight but warming circle
around the floor

and they can leave,
laughing lightly and slamming car doors,
blowing off toward the dropped sun:

we stand back from the windows,
listening to the roses scratch against the house
and to the rustlings of the cat
far down the hall.

He moves first to start the rice.
I have found a new opening
in the wall,
the source perhaps of the faint ribbon of cold air
which drifted in all winter.